For Dad –
with love from Pat

Laurels for Father

Laurels for Father

Great Tributes in Prose and Poetry

Edited by Ralph L. Woods

PUBLISHED BY
THE C. R. GIBSON COMPANY

To Paul R. Huot

The Father of Three Delightful Children

*A complete list of acknowledgments will be
found at the end of the book.*

Preface

I *have been astonished — though I don't quite know why — to encounter so many moving tributes to fathers while researching for this book. Many have been glowing memories of a father's love and companionship. But perhaps more striking — and certainly of equal importance — are the eloquent testimonies of the deep and abiding influence fathers have had on their children.*

Perhaps I have been surprised by these happy discoveries because fathers do not generally talk much about their parental activities; they are much readier to dwell on their child's accomplishments and prospects of surpassing the parent's achievements.

Fathers, it seems, take their children and their responsibilities to them seriously, but fathers do not ordinarily take themselves too seriously. They even spoof themselves.

However, the pages that follow warmly and often poignantly demonstrate that father is not the forgotten man. And as a father it has been a pleasure to have this added assurance.

R.L.W.

CONTENTS

God will not look you over for medals,
degrees or diplomas,
but for scars.

Elbert Hubbard

I

A Father's Love

The Little Child's Faith

It's a comfort to me in life's battle,
  When the conflict seems all going wrong,
When I seem to lose every ambition
  And the current of life grows too strong,
To think that the dusk ends the warfare,
  That the worry is done for the night;
And the little child there, at the window,
  Believes that his daddy's all right.

In the heat of the day and the hurry,
  I'm prompted so often to pause,
While my mind strays away from the striving,
  Away from the noise and applause.
The cheers may be meant for some other;
  Perhaps I have lost in the fight;
But the little child waits at the window,
  Believing his daddy's all right.

I can laugh at the downfalls and failure,
  I can smile in the trial and pain;
I can feel that in spite of the errors,
  The struggle has not been in vain.
If Fortune will only retain me
  That comfort and solace at night,
When the little child waits at the window,
  Believing his daddy's all right.

LOUIS EDWIN THAYER

A wise son maketh a glad father.

PROVERBS 10, 1

Love and Laughter

My father was the sole support of five unusually healthy and hungry children, his frail and clinging little sister Kitty, his wife with her fixed ideas of "niceness," which included fresh tablecloths daily, butter made into balls, children's underlinen changed three times weekly, and, of course, a cook in the kitchen and a young girl to help with beds, child care, and the Monday wash.

Added to these responsibilities was some regular and some emergency help for my mother's family, and the usual suburban outlay for commuters' tickets, carfare, club, lunches, and so on. He bought a surrey and an old horse named Hatrack; he bought a cow my mother really loved, Dolly; he bought an incubator for my brother Joe to manage so that we might always have chicken for Sunday lunch. Just how this was done on the salary paid the manager of a small private bank it is hard to understand now, but he did it, and was always optimistic, content, and ready with Sunday plans for long walks and picnics in Muir Woods over the hill some four miles away. We were always aware of his presence when he was in the house or anywhere about, for his interest in a thousand small things was vigorous and he usually wanted to share it with one of us.

He would read me a passage from Byron or Macaulay, under his green light in the study that was merely an alcove off the big homey sitting room, or he would call Teresa from her absorption in Gayley's *Classic Myths* to come and tell her poor old father that she loved him. Often when my mother finished some brilliant piano performance he would murmur, "Thanks, Jo. Wonderful!" without stopping his reading. Both older sons crossed the Bay with him on their way to school in San Francisco every morning, and as for the smaller children, they built block houses and walked chessmen about his feet, under his table, unrebuked.

Phrases of my father's making have lived long after him. Once, when in the discontented teens I was bewailing the fact, with that faculty all teen-agers have for boring their hearers insufferably, that I was not as good-looking as my sister, mother, or aunts, my father said staunchly, "Well, even if it's so, we can't all be handsome. But I've always felt that a handsome man has only a twenty-minute start on me!" I've remembered this at many a dinner table when a Hollywood beauty happened to be at my host's left.

At another time some members of the home circle accused me of exaggeration. "Let her alone!" said Dad. "Any good story deserves a top hat and a stick!"

And in defense of home hospitalities he quoted his Irish grandfather: "No man was ever carried to the poorhouse on his dining room table!"

KATHLEEN NORRIS

My Little Child

Say of him what you please, but I know my child's failings.

I do not love him because he is good, but because he is my little child.

How should you know how dear he can be when you try to weigh his merits against his faults?

When I must punish him, he becomes all the more a part of my being.

When I cause his tears to come, my heart weeps with him.

I alone have a right to blame and punish, for he only may chastise who loves.

RABINDRANATH TAGORE

The Secret Heart

Across the years he could recall
His father one way best of all.

In the stillest hour of night
The boy awakened to a light.

Half in dream he saw his sire
With his great hands full of fire.

The man had struck a match to see
If his son slept peacefully.

He held his palms each side the spark
His love had kindled in the dark.

His two hands were curved apart
In the semblance of a heart.

He wore, it seemed to his small son,
A bare heart on his hidden one.

A heart that gave out such a glow
No son awake could bear to know.

It showed a look upon a face
Too tender for the day to trace.

One instant, it lit all about,
And then the secret heart went out.

But it shone long enough for one
To know that hands help up the sun.

ROBERT P. T. TRISTRAM COFFIN

One of the advantages in using love to control your children, is that you don't lose control when you get arthritic.

Robert E. Lee as a Father

His tenderness to his children, especially to his daughters, was mingled with a delicate courtesy which belonged to an older day than ours, a courtesy which recalls the *preux chevalier* of knightly times. He had a pretty way of addressing his daughters, in the presence of other people, with a prefix which would seem to belong to the age of lace ruffles and side swords. "Where is my little Miss Mildred?" he would say on coming home from his ride or walk at dusk. "She is my light-bearer; the house is never dark if she is in it."

MARGARET J. PRESTON

Every noble youth looks back, as to the chiefest joy which this world's honor ever gave him, to the moment when first he saw his father's eyes flash with pride, and his mother turn away her head, lest he should take her tears for tears of sorrow.

JOHN RUSKIN

Miniature

My day-old son is plenty scrawny,
His mouth is wide with screams, or yawny,
His ears seem larger than he's needing,
His nose is flat, his chin receding,
His skin is very, very red,
He has no hair upon his head,
And yet I'm proud as proud can be
To hear you say he looks like me.

RICHARD ARMOUR

Like Father, Like Son

We are more like the man, a Yale graduate, who took his son to enroll at the alma mater. He had heard the rumors about new ways and notions there, so he sought out the dean of students and told him his dream for the boy: "I want him to get exactly what I got when I was here." The dean puzzled for a moment and then asked, "You mean you want him to follow in your footsteps?" The father smilingly agreed. The dean said, "Look, now! You're a great guy and we're proud of you, but don't you think one of you is enough."

HAROLD A. BOSLEY

Paternity, a "Psychic Revolution"

The realization that he has passed on the torch of life, and can see it flowering before his eyes in "his own image and likeness," is the basic reason why a man when he becomes a father is no longer just a man. His is the supreme moment of self-recovery, the resigning of a lease on life; it is time's best moment, when a man feels, within himself, the shimmering refraction of the Eternal Joy of an Eternal Father begetting an Eternal Son, and saying to him in the noontide of Paternity: "Thou art my son; I have begotten thee this day." (Psalm 2, 7) . . .

This psychic revolution at the instant of paternity has also a further effect. Not only is it a bond with a child, but it is also a new bond with the mother. The newborn child not only unveiled fatherhood in the husband, but also motherhood in the wife. From that moment on, she appears before him in a relationship which never before existed.

FULTON J. SHEEN

"I Have Found What I Sought."

Many years I lost happiness. I sought it in knowledge, and found disillusionment. I sought it in writing, and found a weariness of the flesh. I sought it in travel, and my feet tired on the way. I sought it in wealth, and I found discord and worriment.

And then one day, at a little station out on a wooded cliff near the sea, I saw a woman waiting in a tiny car, with a child asleep in her arms. A man alighted from the train, walked to her quickly, embraced her, and kissed the child gently, careful lest he should awaken her. They drove off together to some modest house among the fields; and it seemed to me that happiness was with them.

Today I have neglected my writing. The voice of a little girl calling to me, "Come out and play," drew me from my papers and my books. Was it not the final purpose of my toil that I should be free to frolic with her, and spend unharassed hours with the one who had given her to me? And so we walked and ran and laughed together, and fell in the tall grass, and hid among the trees; and I was young again.

Now it is evening; while I write, I hear the child's breathing as she sleeps in her cozy bed. And I know that I have found what I sought. I perceived that if I will do as well as I can the tasks for which life has made me, I shall find fulfillment, and a quiet lane of happiness for many years. Gladly I surrender to nature's imperative of love and parentage, trusting to her ancient wisdom, and knowing that as Dante learned when he entered Paradise, "La sua volontate è nostra pace — In her will and service is our peace."

WILL DURANT

Father's Day at My House

I would as lief nobody got my Father's Day present from any of those for-the-man-who-has-everything stores. I don't want a mink bottle opener or a platinum toothpick or a pair of fluorescent shoelaces or argyle socks for my golf clubs, and I've already got a shrunken head. I'm wearing it now.

I'd much rather get a present from a for-the-man-who-hasn't-anything store, if there is such a place.

Some pipe cleaners, for example, would be especially nice. I mean some pipe cleaners of my *own*. I take home a new package every few days, but Harriet and the kids use them up before I get to them.

Agatha wears them in her hair, wrapped around her pony tail. Harriet fixes them so the ends arch out from Agatha's head like the antennae on a butterfly, and ties tiny little bells to the tips. Agatha looks like some kind of a bug, and the bug hairdo has now become a neighborhood fad.

Cuthbert uses pipe cleaners to hold his model boats and airplanes together while the glue sets.

So when I want a pipe cleaner I have to argue Cuthbert out of one, catch Agatha, or pull the crutch out from under a sick plant. It's simpler to smoke a dirty pipe.

An alarm clock of my very own would be nice, too. We have a good alarm clock in our house, but my son Cuthbert is in charge of it. He has a couple of rabbit traps out, and likes to get up and check them himself before the kids next door do. He sets the clock for 6 A.M., and puts it inside the ten-gallon lard can we use to steam crabs in. For added effects, he puts two or three dozen marbles into the can, too.

The amplification is amazing. The clock doesn't ticktock any more. It goes TWINK-TWANK-TWANK, TWINK, TWANK.

The first time it went off I thought there was a wreck out in front of the house. It's not that frightening, now that we're used to it, but it still sounds like somebody breaking a plate-glass window.

If I had my own alarm-clock, I have often mused wistfully at 2 o'clock in the morning, I could sleep for the rest of the summer out on the porch, which is at the other end of the house from Cuthbert's room.

There are all sorts of other much-needed presents. I'd be delighted with a set of new rubber blades for the windshield wipers on the car. The ones I have now don't wipe water; they just comb it a little.

And I could use one of those tiny pins that hold eyeglasses together at the elbow. This paper clip I'm using isn't going to last forever.

A new calendar for that trick window in my wallet would also be nice.

The only trouble is that I can't make up my mind which present I need the most. Tell you what. While I try to decide on something definite, go ahead and get me another tie.

RALPH REPPERT

By profession I am a soldier and take pride in that fact. But I am prouder to be a father. My hope is that my son, when I am gone, will remember me not from the battle, but in the home, repeating with him one simple prayer, "Our Father which art in heaven."

DOUGLAS MACARTHUR

In the Götterdämmerung which over-wise science and over-foolish statesmen are preparing for us, the last man will spend his last hours searching for his wife and child.

RALPH LINTON

"What a Man Father Was!"

The first clear memory I have of my father is associated with an hour of terror. It was night and dark, and I was alone. Then Father came, lifted me from my crib, held me against his deep, warm chest, and laughed quietly and reassuringly. I had the croup, a scourge in those days, but in Father's comforting arms I relaxed and began to breathe quietly. Instinctively, because Father laughed, I knew that I need not be afraid.

Later, the first time I looked at death, Father again carried me in his arms and made it gentle. The tiny, still form lying in its cradle was my baby sister, Addie. In my lifetime I have seen death approach many times to claim those dear to me or, in the horror of brutal war, to strike down men whose names were unknown to me. But no matter the outward circumstances, the memory of my father's protecting arms always come back to be part of my reassurance, my consolation . . .

In Lafayette, south of Portland [Oregon] in the Willamette Valley, Father built the little church that was the largest and most beautiful building in my small world. Much of the work he did with his own hands, and in the same way he helped build churches elsewhere in his wide parish. Stone upon stone, board above board, I watched our church rise, and then I saw it painted — white for the body, the tower in several colors. I played in the shadow of its walls and later worshipped at its altar. The faith my father declared from the pulpit he nailed together became my faith . . .

The preacher who built the white church, and who filled it with the sermons of his faith, came back to it often for more than sixty years. I heard him last in that pulpit when he was nearly ninety. Today the little church bears his name and is a memorial to him and to the woman who stood by his side and largely made him what he became . . .

What a man Father was! Even in near-poverty he could inspire his sons with the attractiveness of his high calling. Like Mother, he never really grew old. Sickness, major operations, and the inevitable disappointments of life left him still the incurable optimist. When he was past eighty-five he put a new roof on his house in Portland. It had been my joy and privilege to give the house to my parents. Father loved his house. As we surveyed the finished job, he was clearly not pleased. "I made a mistake," he told me. "Those synthetic shingles look all right, but an Oregon house should be covered with clear cedar, and that's what I'll put on next." . . .

Father lived into his ninetieth year . . . Father's last words — they were written down for me — were: "I know that I am a dying man but I am a victorious man. I have a message for the Conference. Preach Christ, preach Christ crucified, buried and risen from the dead." Self-denying, ageless, indomitable Father — as he slipped away his thoughts turned from himself to his church, and his words were like the climax of a last sermon.

DANIEL A. POLING

Robert G. Ingersoll to His Daughter, on Her Thirty-fourth Birthday.

Sept. 22nd, 1897

Dear Eva,

Thirty-four years of unbroken kindness, of cloudless sunshine, of perpetual joy, of constant love. Thirty-four years of happy smiles, of loving looks, of gentle words, of generous deeds. Thirty-four years of perfect days — perfect as the heart of June. Thirty-four years, a flower, a palm, a star; a faultless child, a perfect woman, wife and mother.

"Yay, Daddy!"

Anthropologists think it is a Bad Thing to teach cheer-leading to our coeds instead of more cultural matters. There is something in what they say. Still, don't our burgeoning women need at least some training in the fundamentals of enthusiasm? They don't get much of it in the classical curriculum.

A young woman goes to college and she takes a course in Shakespeare. This teaches her to be critical. She looks through the works of the Bard and spots every little understandable mistake he makes, like having a clock tick in *Julius Caesar* . . .

Criticism is an important part of the well-rounded girl, but I am not sure that it is the most essential quality she can bring to a marriage. The average husband does not need somebody to point out that it was a mistake for him to put the ladder through the window while removing the screens . . .

The cheerleader reacts to mistakes in a different way than does the Shakespearean scholar. When the quarter-back passes the ball to the other team on his own five-yard line, she does not call for a chorus of boos and nit-picking. Instead she shrieks, "Hit 'em again harder" or "We want a touchdown" . . .

The advantage of a liberal education is that it imparts an objective attitude toward the vast issues which crash and thunder around the ears of the citizen. But the husband needs partisanship more than he does objectivity. He is out there every day struggling against an opposing team that has him outweighed, outthought and outnumbered.

When he gets home at night, he doesn't need a well-reasoned discussion of himself versus the establishment. He wants someone who will meet him at the door and cry to the kids:

"Let's hear it for Daddy. Two steamrollers and a tiger. D-A-D-D-Y. Yay, DADDY!"

When he leaves in the morning, full of self-doubts as to how the uneven contest will go, it would help if a "Fight! Fight! Fight!" were ringing in his ears.

BILL VAUGHAN

FATHER: A man whose daughter marries a man vastly her inferior mentally, but then gives birth to unbelievably brilliant grandchildren.

The Blind Boy

I know what my father's face is like;
*   I'm sure I know it all;*
It's like his whistle on the air;
It's like his arms which take such care
*   And never let me fall.*

ANONYMOUS

The Larger World

I remember that at eight years old I walked with him [his father] one winter evening from a farmer's house . . . and he told me the names of the stars and how Jupiter was a thousand times larger than our world, and that the other twinkling stars were suns that had worlds rolling around them; and when I came home he showed me how they rolled round. I heard him with a profound delight and admiration; but without the least mixture of wonder or incredulity . . . I know no other way of giving the mind a love of the Great and the Whole.

SAMUEL TAYLOR COLERIDGE

The Joy of Fatherhood

Much is written in poetic praise of motherhood. Little is written in that vein of fatherhood. The father is generally regarded as a kind of noble but weary beast of burden, silently enduring the tedium of providing for his family. Of the rewards of fatherhood almost nothing is said. Yet I suspect that the most gigantic of all human joys are experienced by fathers.

My own father used to embarrass me by the way in which he looked at me. It was as if I were something too wonderful to be true, merely because I was there. I felt that if he were to utter what was in his heart, I would be covered with confusion at the vision of the marvel of my own existence. But of course he could not utter it. He simply looked at me, and at the other children, as if he were asking how he — inconsequential he — could be the father of beings so mysterious and marvelous.

That was humility; but it was realism, too. Humility may be defined as right realism. And humility is necessary for joy. A man will hardly appreciate a sunset if he imagines, in his pride, that he can paint something better. A woman will not rejoice in a rose if she thinks she can make a more beautiful rose of crepe paper. And a father will not be happy in his children unless he realizes that they come from God, that they are held in existence from moment to moment by the power of God, and that but for God they would vanish in an instant into nothingness.

I wonder whether there can be a father so unappreciative as not to have felt, from time to time, a pang of unutterable happiness in his children, like a wound in the heart. These moments come and go. But I have felt tears of joy in my eyes at the sight of the sturdy straight back of one of my boys, or in the presence of a small daughter's smile.

There is a scene that I have seen several times; and to have seen it once would have repaid me immeasurably for every effort I have invested in fatherhood. It was the sight of a small boy, my son, and a small girl, my daughter, walking hand in hand into the twilight. Symphonies could be written about that. The greatest poets and dramatists could exhaust themselves attempting to express it in words. But it is unutterable. . . .

I don't know what other fathers may feel, but I know what I feel at such moments. I feel that I am shouting together with all the sons of God. . . .

This vision of the privilege of existence, and of the pricelessness of fatherhood, may come upon a man at any moment.

JOSEPH A. BREIG

A Father's Promise

Ebenezer Webster, one of the earliest settlers in New Hampshire, had ten children, including Daniel, a frail child. The family decided that Daniel should be prepared for school teaching. When the mother suggested that if the boys promised to provide for the parents in their old age, she would agree, if necessary, to sell every acre of their land to pay for the sons' education. The startled father finally consented to this.

"I remember," *recalled Daniel Webster later*, "the very hill which we were ascending, through deep snows, in a New England sleigh, when my father made known this promise to me. I could not speak. How could he, I thought, with so large a family, and in such narrow circumstances, think of incurring so great an expense for me? A warm glow ran all over me, and I laid my head on my father's shoulder and wept."

And so Daniel Webster went on to Dartmouth and to fame.

Happy Meeting

There are many little incidents stored in my memory which now waken into life. Especially, I remember that first evening of my return from Oxford in 1818, after gaining the scholarship at Trinity, and my Father saying "What a happy meeting this!" Often and often such sayings of his come to my mind, and almost overpower me; for I consider he did very much for me at a painful sacrifice to himself, and was so generous and kind.

JOHN HENRY NEWMAN

A Common Bond

In December 1943 a New York editor flew in from Europe. In the elevator he met Tony, the little man who shined shoes. He seemed to have shrunken and the editor hardly recognized him. "Why Tony," he said, "you look like the world has fallen in on you." Tony nodded and replied, "Yes, the envelope, it came last night from Washington. Little Tony is dead."

There was silence until the returning editor broke it by asking Tony to get off on his floor and take care of him first. With strict attention to his job Tony created the shine for which he was famous, but there was silence between the two men until the job was finished. Then the editor told the bootblack about his own son who was not coming back, as the two men stood side by side at the office window overlooking Manhattan. When he had finished, Tony's hand touched the editor's hand and as he returned the coin which he had just earned, his face wore the old smile and he spoke with the warmth of his native Italy. "Now we have something together," he said.

DANIEL A. POLING

King George VI to Princess Elizabeth
after Her Marriage to Philip

. . . I was so proud of you and thrilled at having you so close to me on our long walk in Westminster Abbey, but when I handed your hand to the Archbishop I felt I had lost something very precious. You were so calm and composed during the Service and said your words with such conviction, that I knew everything was all right.

I am so glad you wrote and told Mummy that you think the long wait before your engagement and the long time before the wedding was for the best. I was rather afraid that you had thought I was being hardhearted about it. I was so anxious for you to come to South Africa as you know. Our family, us four, the "Royal Family" must remain together with additions of course at suitable moments! I have watched you grow up all these years with pride under the skillful direction of Mummy, who as you know is the most marvellous person in the World in my eyes and I can, I know, always count on you, and now Philip, to help us in our work. Your leaving us has left a great blank in our lives but do remember that your old home is still yours and do come back as much and as often as possible. I can see that you are sublimely happy with Philip which is right but don't forget us is the wish of

Your ever loving and devoted

Papa.

[late November or early December, 1947]

The richest tributes a child can lay at his parent's feet are the little troubles he brings them to share.

BURTON HILLIS

Children are a great comfort in your old age — and they help you reach it faster too.

LIONEL M. KAUFFMAN

Emerson to His Daughter
on the Birth of a Grandson

Concord

Evening

[July 11, 1866]

My dear Edith,

Happy wife and Mother that you are — and not the less surely that the birth of your babe touches this old house and its people and neighbors with unusual joy. I hope the best gifts and graces of his father and mother will combine for this blossom, and highest influences hallow and ripen the firm and perfect fruit. There is nothing in this world so serious as the advent of a child with all his possibilities to parents with good minds and hearts. Fair fall the little boy — he has come among good people. . . . I please myself already that his Fortunes will be worthy of these great days of his country, that he will not be frivolous, that he will be noble and true, and will know what is sacred. . . .

Your loving father,

R. W. EMERSON

No man believes genius is hereditary until he has a son.

A man with seven children is usually more satisfied than a man with a million dollars. The father of seven doesn't want any more.

"I 've never had a bit of trouble with my six fine boys," said the proud father. "The only time I've ever laid a hand on them was in self-defense."

Abraham Lincoln as a Father in Illinois

Mrs. Wallace [Mrs. Lincoln's sister] thinks "Mr. Lincoln was a domestic man by nature." He was not fond of other people's children, but was extremely fond of his own; he was patient, indulgent, and generous with them to a fault. On Sundays he often took those that were large enough, and walked with them into the country, and giving himself up entirely to them, rambled through the green fields or the cool woods, amusing and instructing them for a whole day at a time.

WARD HILL LAMON

The average household consists of a husband who makes the money, and a wife and kids who make it necessary.

*It is not what he has, or even what he does
which expresses the worth of a man,
but what he is.*

Henri Amiel

III

A Father's Integrity

From the Diary of a
Fifteen-year Old Boy in Oklahoma

I should like to be as much like my father as I can, for he is the wisest and kindest and most tolerant man in the world, I do believe. ... Both men and women love my father, for he has great wit and humor and he can keep a whole room roaring with laughter at his sallies, and I have never heard him speak ill of a woman ever; nor does he speak ill of men either except to ridicule to their faces those who are tight-fisted and mean-spirited and whom he has caught in some hypocrisy or meanness like usury or taking advantage of the poor and helpless, whereat he is courageous and his tongue is so sharp and stinging that the man is humiliated. ...

If my father were susceptible to bribery he would be rich, for that politicians, knowing how much influence he has with voters because all those who know him consult him as an oracle, because he is wise and just and all his many friends vote like him, the crooked politicians would pay him in coin or position for his influence. They have sought him, but my father always gives them a tongue-lashing and never allows them to get nearer to his house than the front porch, saying to them that since they are not worthy of his friendship, they may not pass his threshold, and on one occasion when a pompous politician came into our yard without being asked while my father was watering the lawn and sought my father's support, my father called to him as he was entering the gate, "I am not in the market for any Peruna today," and when the fellow came on after that rebuff my father turned the hose on him, and the fellow fled. They are afraid of my father, too, because he is six feet tall and as straight and strong as an Indian runner.

BURTON RASCOE

Father Forgets

Listen, son, I am saying this to you as you lie asleep, one little paw crumpled under your cheek and the blond curls stickily wet on your damp forehead. I have stolen into your room alone. Just a few moments ago, as I sat reading my paper in the library, a hot, stifling wave of remorse swept over me. I could not resist it. Guiltily I came to your bedside.

These were the things I was thinking, son, I had been cross to you. I scolded you as you were dressing for school because you gave your face merely a dab with a towel. I took you to task for not cleaning your shoes. I called out angrily when I found you had thrown some of your things on the floor.

At breakfast, I found fault, too. You spilled things. You gulped down your food. You put your elbows on the table. You spread butter too thick on your bread. And as you started off to play and I made for my train, you turned and waved a little and called, "Good-bye, Papa!" and I frowned and said in reply, "Hold your shoulders back!"

Then it began all over again in the late afternoon. As I came up the hill road, I spied you, down on your knees, playing marbles. There were holes in your stockings. I humiliated you before your boy friends, by making you march on ahead of me, back to the house. Stockings were expensive — and if *you* had to buy them you would be more careful. Imagine that, son, from a father! It was such a stupid, silly logic.

But do you remember later, when I was reading in the library, how you came in softly, timidly, with a sort of hurt, hunted look in your eyes? When I glanced up, over my paper, impatient at the interruption, you hesitated at the door.

"What is it you want?" I snapped.

You said nothing, but you ran across, gathering all your childish courage, in one tempestuous plunge, and threw your arms around my neck, and kissed me, again and again, and your small arms tightened with an affection that God had set blooming in your heart and which even neglect could not wither. And then you were gone, pattering up the stairs.

Well, son, it was shortly afterwards that my paper slipped from my hands and a terrible, sickening fear came over me. Suddenly I saw myself as I really was, in all my horrid selfishness, and I felt sick at heart.

What had habit been doing to me? The habit of complaining, of finding fault, of reprimanding — all these were my rewards to you for being a boy. It was not that I did not love you; it was that I expected so terribly much of youth. I was measuring you by the yardstick of my own years.

And there is so much that is good, and fine, and true in your character. You did not *deserve* my treatment of you, son. The little heart of you was as big as the dawn itself, over wide hills. All this was shown by your spontaneous impulse to rush in and kiss me goodnight. Nothing else matters, tonight, son. I have come to your bedside in the darkness, and I have knelt here, choking with emotion and so ashamed! . . .

And I have prayed God to strengthen me in my new resolve. Tomorrow I will be a *real* daddy! I will chum with you and suffer when you suffer and laugh when you laugh, I will bite my tongue when impatient words come. I will keep saying, as if it were a ritual: "He is nothing but a boy — a little boy!"

WILLIAM LIVINGSTON LARNED

A Father is a banker provided by nature.

Only a Dad

Only a dad with a tired face,
Coming home from the daily race.
Bringing little of gold or fame
To show how well he has played the game;
But glad in his heart that his own rejoice
To see him come and to hear his voice.

Only a dad with a brood of four,
One of ten million men or more
Plodding along in the daily strife,
Bearing the whips and the scorns of life,
With never a whimper of pain or hate,
For the sake of those who at home await.

Only a dad, neither rich nor proud,
Merely one of the surging crowd,
Toiling, striving from day to day,
Facing whatever may come his way,
Silent whenever the harsh condemn,
And bearing it all for the love of them.

Only a dad but he gives his all,
To smooth the way for his children small,
Doing with courage stern and grim
The deeds that his father did for him.
This is the line that for him I pen:
Only a dad, but the best of men.

EDGAR A. GUEST

Many fathers will agree with the wit who said: "When I was young my parents told me what to do; now my children tell me what to do. I wonder when I'll be able to do what I want to do?"

What greater ornament to a son than a father's glory, or to a father than a son's honorable conduct.

SOPHOCLES, *Antigone*

Thomas Carlyle to His Mother, on the Death of His Father

I trusted that I might have other glad meetings and pleasant communings with my honored and honorworthy father in this world, but it was not so appointed. We shall meet no more till we meet in that *other* sphere where God's Presence more immediately is. . . .

One other comfort we have to take the bitterness out of our tears — this greatest of all comforts, and properly the only one: that our father was not called away till he had done his work, and done it faithfully. Yes, we can with holy pride look at our father there where he lies low, and say that his task was well and manfully performed; the strength that God had given him he put forth in the ways of honesty and well-doing; no eye will ever see a hollow, deceitful work that *he* did; the world wants one true man since he was taken away. When we consider his life, through what hardships and obstructions he struggled, and what he became and what he did, there is room for gratitude that God so bore him on. Oh, what were it now to us that he had been a king? now, when the question is not, What *wages* hadst thou for thy work? How was thy work done?

None of us but started life with *far* greater advantages than our dear father had; we will not weep for him, but we will go and do as he has done. Could I write my books as he built his houses, and walk my way so manfully through this shadowy world, and leave it with so little blame, it were more than all my hopes.

"It Was a Glory Walking Down Main Street."

Turning Papa loose in Oklahoma, Indian Territory, in 1906, was like taking a house cat that had never known more than a corner of a kitchen and letting it run wild in an acre of catnip. Mama's family in Texas had bottled him up until neither he nor they could take each other. Suddenly he was free to call his shots in a new country where every settler had an equal chance. Overnight Max Meyer blew the cork out of the bottle that had restrained him, and grew into a giant of a man.

Papa fell in love with the confusion that existed on every street and in every building in Sapulpa. He took on the friendly braggadocio of the natives, who were new-comers a month before. The constantly changing scene excited him. . . .

Papa looked like an Indian. Traveling salesmen always asked him what tribe he belonged to. "The Lost Tribe" he'd answer with just enough of a straight face to throw them for a loss. Papa's store in fact was unofficial headquarters for the Five Civilized Tribes. Indians liked him and trusted him. More than one merchant said, "Get an Indian drunk and you can sell him anything." Papa worked on another theory: get an Indian sober and he'll be your friend. Many Indians came to Papa's store when their money was gone and their hangovers coming on. Indian women, in their blankets of bright, beautiful colors, spent hours in the shoe department while their men slept off their binges on cots Papa installed for that purpose in a corner of his Bargain Basement.

In his store safe he kept Indians' marriage licenses, army discharges, car registrations, and often considerable sums of cash. He was proud that the Indians trusted him more than they did the bank. . . .

It was a glory walking down Main Street with Papa. He was king, general, conquering hero, vote getter, super-salesman, father confessor, and Trumpeter of the Morn. Whether he was walking to the post office for the morning mail, walking to the bank to talk about a check of his that had bounced, walking to the Farmer's Exchange for a midmorning snack of raw carrots and new peas, or walking to the courthouse jail to bail out Ernie Cooper, you had the feeling that the walk itself was as important to Papa as the errand to be done at the end of it.

What did he *say*?

He said, "Good *mornin'*, Mrs. Springer! Your hair is pure gold in the mornin' sun!" Mrs. Springer flipped with happiness. He said, "Get out of that car and use your legs, Harold Lane! Who wants to drive on a day like this?" He'd spy ancient Mrs. Anderson, a fragile, pink-and-white old lady whose husband, a driller of wild-cat wells, had killed himself after a siege of dry holes. He'd make a sweeping bow from the waist, courtier-fashion, and croon, "Ah, Mrs. Anderson, it's the kind of day that makes a person want to live forever . . . and I hope you do!" He'd shout to friends in cars. He'd bugle at people in stores. He'd wave. He'd point. People looked at him, even when they were unaware they were looking. Whenever he went away on a buying trip for the store, Main Street drooped.

LEWIS MEYER

In my dealing with my child, my accomplishments and my money stead me nothing; but as much soul as I have avails. If I am wilful, he sets his will against mine, one for one, and leaves me, if I please, the degradation of beating him by my superiority of strength. But if I renounce my will and act for the soul, setting that up as umpire between us two, out of his young eyes looks the same soul; he reveres and loves with me.

RALPH WALDO EMERSON

"He Was Made of the Martyr's Stuff."

This was the kind of man my mother met at a dance in Emporia [Kansas] in the fall of 1865. He was forty-six years old; not much taller than she, probably five feet five and one half inches, he weighed two hundred and twenty pounds. ... He had a hard, tough mind. He was a thrifty young man, but apparently he made money easily, saved it without much agony or compunction. ...

His indignation had a low boiling point, but he was also a stayer and a sticker and loved to walk with a minority. He was a Democrat during the war. They called him a Copperhead because he believed in a negotiated peace. ... He endured during four years of war all the contumely a man must endure in a community where every able-bodied man was a soldier at war and he, who was undersized, overweight and had lost the trigger finger on his right hand and was just over-aged, remained at home. In the town and county they always said, even the G.A.R. boys when they came back patronizing him heavily, that "old Doc White" never charged the wife or children of a soldier at the front for any services while the war was on, which made his practice pretty much charity.

He loved medicine but never could make it pay because he did not keep his collections up. So every few years, being a Yankee and a natural trader, he would retire from practice and make some money, pay his debts, get a little ahead, and then go at medicine again. For he was made of the martyr's stuff, though he had in his heart an eternal wellspring of good nature, good humor and good jokes. ...

I should have been heartbroken at the loss of my father. I was not. After the first few hours or days of acute grief, I went about my business and resented the tender solicitude of those who supposed I would be mourning deeply. Yet I know now, and probably knew then, that he was a good father to me and a good man in all his relations. I never saw him lose his temper more than once; and that was only for a second and he was penitent about it for a day or two. He never spanked me or administered any corporal punishment. If I had any, it was when I was too young to remember it; and my mother doubtless did the job anyway, for she flew off the handle easily. I know now that my father was always trying to tell me about himself — about his boyhood. Being a boy, I could not realize what he was doing so sedulously. It all slipped away from me, though I am sure that, spiritually, he made me — not by blood inheritance so much as by the unconscious guidance he gave me, the example he set, which I know now I tried to follow, and by the practical ideals he established. He was tolerant but never uncertain of his convictions, which he held courageously but never cantankerously. He hated argument and wrangling. Above everything, he was humorously self-deprecating, perhaps even consciously clowning a bit. ... He must either laugh at himself or strut. And I am sure that strutting would have irked him and he would have laughed himself out of his own pomposity. ...

All of his books . . . I read. When I begin to look back at them and see my father in perspective, I realize that he was in some ways an exceptional man who sought real leadership and tried to keep it anonymous; who loved power but always pretended he had none; who made money easily and spent it wisely and never had a miserly desire to be rich. I know that one of his hidden vanities was to be the first man on the subscription paper with the largest donation. ...

A boy of fourteen could not comprehend such a man as he was. But when my memory puts him together again, I could mourn him deeply. I have never ceased to sorrow that he did not stay with me for another twenty

years, to help me and to guide me from the follies which
he may have seen ahead of me. I know now what I did
not know then — that I was the apple of his eye. He
loved me and hoped for me and maybe, to whatever gods
he knew, he prayed for me. And when I was old I did
not depart from the way!

WILLIAM ALLEN WHITE

Dad

Dad never had much to say;
Jogged along in his quiet way
Contentedly smoking his old dudeen
As he turned the soil to the golden sheen.
Used to say as he slapped the mare,
One horny hand in his tangled hair,
"Rest is joy when your work's well done,
So pitch in, son."

Sometimes he an' I'd not hitch;
Couldn't agree as to which was which.
Fought it out on the same old lines
As we grubbed an' hoed 'mong the runnin' vines;
And his eyes would light with a gentle quiz,
And he'd say in that old soft way of his,
As he idly stroked his wrinkled chin.
"All right, son, you win."

WILLIAM E. ROSS

Father! — to God himself we cannot give
A holier name!

WILLIAM WORDSWORTH

What Is a Father?

A father is a thing that is forced to endure childbirth, without an anesthetic.

A father is a thing that growls when it feels good — and laughs when it's scared half to death.

He never feels entirely worthy of the worship in a child's eyes. He's never quite the hero his daughter thinks — never quite the man his son believes him to be — and this worries him, sometimes. So he works too hard to try and smooth the rough places in the road for those of his own who will follow him.

Fathers grow old faster than people. Because they have to stand at the train station and wave good-bye to the uniform that climbs aboard. And while mothers can cry where it shows, fathers have to stand there and beam outside — and die inside.

Fathers have very stout hearts, so they have to be broken sometimes or no one would know what's inside.

Fathers are what give daughters away to other men who aren't nearly good enough — so they can have grand-children that are smarter than anybody's.

Fathers fight dragons — almost daily. They hurry away from the breakfast table; off to the arena which is sometimes called an office or a workshop. There, with calloused, practiced hands they tackle the dragon with three heads: Weariness, Work, and Monotony. And they never quite win the fight but they never give up.

Knights in shining armor — fathers in shiny trousers — there's little difference, as they march away to work each workday.

ANONYMOUS

A man can say what he pleases in his own home because no one pays any attention to him.

A Famous Father and Son

Up the Hudson at Pocantico Hills (on a beautiful estate), near Tarrytown, New York, lives a retired country gentleman who has passed his eighty-ninth birthday. ... Never a lover of luxury, but precise in his requirements as to convenience and orderliness, he is a character of unique simplicity. ... He is John D. Rockefeller. ...

Down at 26 Broadway in lower Manhattan, sitting at the center of a long table in an oak-paneled room, is a man of fifty-five, solidly built, five feet seven or eight inches in height, with square shoulders, cleancut features, wide forehead, firm lips, and a determined chin. Like his father, John D. Rockefeller, Jr., rises at seven o'clock, leaving home so as to be at his office between half-past eight and nine. ...

Now, between these two men, who so strikingly resemble each other in their methodical way of doing things, there has existed for half a century one of the most remarkable paternal and filial relationships that history records. Furthermore, it is safe to say that no man, without qualification or definite stipulation, has ever reposed in his son such complete trust in matters of vast import and involving such huge sums as the elder Rockefeller has done.

Some years ago, when the list of stockholders in the various Standard Oil companies was made public, many financiers were surprised to learn that most of the Rockefeller holdings were owned not by the father but by his only son. ... The senior Rockefeller had come to the conclusion that, since his son was carrying most of the burden, he ought to have control of their interests. In consequence, he had turned over to his son several hundred million dollars in securities at one time. ...

"I cannot remember when hard work was new or strange to me," the elder Rockefeller has said; and it was in this same school that his son was brought up.

"So far as money was concerned," said Mr. Rockefeller, Jr., "we children came to realize that there was nothing we could not have, had Father been disposed to give it to us. There were other children who had a great deal more than we had. . . .

"We were taught that we should work to earn the pleasures we enjoyed. We learned to work, to save and to give; but there was nothing rigid about the system by which we were taught this. . . . If one of us saved ten dollars, then Father was ready to put ten dollars more with it to go into the bank.

"School work did not come easily to me, and I was determined to do the best I could. Father never expected more than that, but he did expect *that*. Whatever my marks, even if I was far behind from the head of the class, I was never censured if I had done my best."

Upon being graduated [from college] in 1897 . . . he came to the conclusion that, as his father was then nearing sixty, he could not afford the time either for law or for travel. Immediately after his summer vacation, he went into his father's office. . . .

"Father said not a word to me about what I was to do in the office before I went to work there, nor has he ever since. Moreover, he did not say anything on that subject to anyone else in the office, so far as I have ever learned. Apparently, it was his intention that I should make my own way.

"To begin with, I studied the books of accounts, acquainting myself with the affairs of the office generally. . . . I sat in various conferences and business meetings, listening and learning as much as I could from my father's business associates." . . .

As the younger Rockefeller came more in touch with affairs, he signed various agreements and important papers for his father; but he did not sign as his father's attorney, never having been given any power of attorney nor any specific authorization in these matters.

"Someone had to sign these papers," Mr. Rockefeller remarked. "I knew that the matters referred to were in accord with my father's wishes, and simply assumed the authority to act. ... I felt that he trusted me and knew I had only one desire — to help him to the full extent of my ability, and so I took the chance of acting without orders. ... It was evidently Father's idea that I should learn that I could make a place for myself if I were able to do so."

M. K. WISEHART

The highest example of justice, as Jesus saw, is not a judge but a father, who knows his children separately and considers what is right for each one of them, and looks always to their good and happiness. God is righteous because He is like a father.

E. F. SCOTT

Ernie Pyle Tells about His Father

Perhaps you have heard of my father. He is the man who put oil on his brakes when they got to squeaking, then drove to Dana [Indiana] and ran over the curb and through a plate-glass window and right into a dry-goods store.

My father is also the man who ran with Roosevelt in 1932. He ran for township trustee, was the only Democrat in the county who lost, and was probably the happiest man who listened to election returns that night. He couldn't think of anything worse than being township trustee. The reason he lost was that all the people figured that if he was trustee he wouldn't have time to put roofs on their houses and paint their barns and paper their dining rooms and fix their chimneys, and do a thousand and one other things for them. I guess when my father is gone that whole neighborhood will just sort of fall down.

He used to work as a hired hand on the other side of the Wabash River. When he was courting my mother, every Sunday he would drive a horse six miles to the river, row a boat across, and then ride a bicycle ten miles to my mother's house. At midnight he started to reverse the process. Mother figured he either loved her or else was foolish and needed somebody to look after him; so she married him.

My father had never lived anywhere except on a farm, and yet I don't think he ever did like the farm very well. He has been happiest, I think, since he started renting out the farm. Ever since then he has been carpentering and handy-manning all about the neighborhood. He is a wizard with tools, where other people are clumsy. He is a carpenter at heart. . . .

He is a very quiet man. He has never said a great deal to me all his life, and yet I feel we have been very good friends. He never gave me much advice, or told me to do this or that, or not to. He bought me a Ford roadster when I was about sixteen, and when I wrecked it a couple of weeks later he never said a word. But he didn't spare me either; I worked like a horse from the time I was nine.

He never showed much emotion, and he has never seen a big-league ball game. Yet my mother came home one afternoon during a World Series, and caught him sitting in front of the radio, all by himself, and yelling for all he was worth.

My father is now getting a little deaf. Mother says he can always hear what he isn't supposed to hear. If my father doesn't like people, he never says anything about it. He is very even-tempered. If he has an enemy in the whole county, I have yet to hear about it.

He doesn't swear or drink or smoke. He is honest, in letter and in spirit. He is a good man without being at all annoying about it.

Father Confers with the Teacher

I resent parent conferences. I resent the teacher and I resent my kid. I even resent my wife's placid attitude toward these affairs. The instant she and I walk through the door and I see the teacher smiling frostily at us, my blood curdles and I regret that schools were ever invented.

I know that my little hellion, my boy, is not going to break the Otis quick-scoring thermometer. But he is my guy, and the same kind of brains pretty much run in the family. That's exactly the point. It's nobody's business what brains run in my family. They're the only brains we have, and we're stuck with them.

Therefore, I approach the teacher with my head up. I look her squarely in the eye, perhaps as long as half a second.

"Well," I say defiantly, dipping into the cavernous depths of my courage.

"Won't you be seated?" she leers at my wife and me.

There is nothing for us to do but obey her by squeezing ourselves into primary grade seats.

"I, that is, we, the both of us, in holy bond of matrimony," I say, all verbal thumbs, "have come henceforth here, to listen, that is, discuss the situation relative to the product of our union."

"You have an interesting little fellow," she says. "No doubt a chip off the old block."

There! Already she's broken a basic principle of Anglo-Saxon jurisprudence. I am presumably guilty before I've had an opportunity to defend myself. If I had any sense at all, I'd call off the conference instantly, until I could get a competent lawyer. But it's too late. Court has convened. The prosecutor, judge, and jury has opened her case.

Extending a pink claw, she reaches for a folder — Exhibit A in the case of the School v. Father and Son.

"His art work," she says, handing me the folder.

"Never was much of an artist myself," I reply.

"Drawings," she says, "are often an indication of personality. Now if you'll notice the large door he's sketched."

"I've been meaning to fix the front door for some time. I think it's the moisture from the ground. The door's too close to the ground."

The teacher mumbles something about big doors indicating security and open-heartedness. I'm not buying any of that. I know her type. Sly at first — then wham!

"Now here are some of his papers in arithmetic."

See! First the soft buildup, a light tap to the chin, then the old haymaker. I can see through the whole scheme.

"The mathematical mind doesn't run in our family," I explain hastily. "We're given more to linguistics, you know. Not linguistics exactly, but perhaps socio-linguistics. Or perhaps socio-dramatics. . . ."

"Well, that is interesting. I rather supposed he got his knack for numbers from his father."

"Not at all," I say. "Knack? What knack?"

"Perhaps, then, he has his father's skill for reading."

"Skill, did you say?" I mumbled.

"Yes, says the teacher, "because he is catching on extremely well. He's so likeable, too . . . a pleasure to have him in the group. You should be very proud of him."

As I was saying, I'm 100 percent in favor of parent conferences. Yes, sir. An openhearted lad. With a knack for numbers. And his father's skill at reading. A real chip off the old block. A shrewd teacher, that one, if I do say so.

CHARLES H. WILSON

The universe is but one great city,
full of beloved ones,
divine and human by nature,
endeared to each other.

Epictetus

A Father's Inspiration

My Father

Because of him I cannot say this world
  Is weary, or a failure, or a fraud,
Or that a lovely vessel must be flawed,
  Or that the hopeful mind is not as brave
As any splendid action that we did laud.

Because of him I cannot say the fall
  Is sad, or that the winter is too hard,
Or that the spring by transiency is marred,
  Or that the summer in its natural fields
Already by the coming frost is scarred.

Because of him whose mind is more my sire
  Than body, and whose heart has been my grace,
I cannot say that man, whom years efface,
  Is not the strong effacer in the end
Of all that's selfish, trivial, and base.

VIRGINIA MOORE

The Soul of Goodness and Truth

My father had never lost his temper with us, never beaten us, but we had for him that feeling often described as fear, which is something quite different and far deeper than alarm. It was that sense which, without irreverence, I have thought to find expressed by the great evangelists when they speak of the fear of God. One does not fear God because he is terrible, but because he is literally the soul of goodness and truth, because to do him wrong is to do wrong to some mysterious part of oneself, and one does not know exactly what the consequences may be.

JOYCE CARY

My Father's Three Words

Three words of my father's that changed my life I can never forget. On a street car he spoke them, between two clangs of the motorman's bell, three words to help and hearten a teen-age boy. They help and hearten him still.
. . .

My dad was a blacksmith in the south Boston car barn; and I myself at 16, confused and unhappy, a junior at the Jesuit High School. My parents were the only ones who thought me capable of college, and they only prayerfully and in spite of the letter I had brought home from the prefect of studies.

Dismayed by my midyear exams, the good Jesuit Father had sent in haste for my dad. . . . Well I remember that fateful night, with the letter waiting for dad to read. For over forty years I can see our kitchen, and the supper waiting while he read the letter. When he'd done, he said, "Never mind the stew, Mary, we'd best get started. Put your rubbers on, Richard, it's beginning to snow."

At 8 o'clock we were there, in the rectory of the Jesuit church, listening to the prefect of studies. The young Father spoke gently, telling of my poor school work, questioning the wisdom of keeping me in high school. "After all, Mr. Cushing," he said, "God calls his children to many vocations; a comparatively few to the life of the intellect, and fewer still to the dignity of his priesthood."

Big and straight in his chair, my father listened, his best hat in his lap, firmly held with both hands. Only once, and quietly, he spoke in my defense, "It could be, Father, he's been working too hard, week-ends and evenings for Father Twomey." And with modest pride, he added, "Assistant janitor, you might say, a good boy and willing."

"No question of that," said the young priest, rising, "nor must you feel bad about it at all. St. Joseph was a carpenter. God will find work for this Richard of yours."

My father thanked him. Then, "Good night, Father," was all he said.

As if it were yesterday, I recall the cold wet dark of the car stop, and the rain that was snow in the oncoming lights of our southbound car. We rode homeward not talking, each with his own thoughts, and mine unhappy. At last I said, pretending indifference as boys will, "They can have their diploma. I'll get a job and help at home."

Dad answered me quietly, words I missed in the crowded aisle. Then three I didn't miss, clearly heard between two clangs of the motorman's bell. *Carry on, son,* he said.

And when we got off at City Point, a few words more. My immigrant father, inarticulate often, but to me that dark night the best of my teachers. Hurrying homeward, "Do the best you can," he told me, "'Tis all God asks. He'll do the rest." Commonplace words, but who knows better to help and hearten child or man, teen-ager or bishop?

"Carry on," said my father long ago. With God's help I will — we will, His children, you and I. My father's three words I pass on to other young lads who find the going rather difficult.

RICHARD CARDINAL CUSHING

To My Father

It matters not that Time has shed
His thawless snow upon your head,
For he maintains, with wondrous art,
Perpetual summer in your heart.

WILLIAM HAMILTON HAYNE

Sir Walter Scott as a Parent

He had now two boys and two girls; and he never had more. He was not one of those who take much delight in a mere infant; but no father ever devoted more time and tender care to his offspring than he did to each of his, as they successively reached the age when they could listen to him, and understand his talk. Like their mute playmates, Camp and the greyhounds, they had at all times free access to his study: he never considered their tattle as any disturbance; they went and came as pleased their fancy; he was always ready to answer their questions; and when they, unconscious how he was engaged, entreated him to lay down his pen and tell them a story, he would take them on his knee, repeat a ballad or a legend, kiss them, and set them down again to their marbles or tenpins, and resume his labor as if refreshed by the interruption. From a very early age he made them dine at table, and "to sit up to supper" was the great reward when they had been "very good bairns." In short, he considered it as the highest duty as well as the sweetest pleasure of a parent to be the companion of his children; he partook of all their little joys and sorrows, and made his kind unformal instructions to blend so easily and playfully with the current of their own sayings and doing, that so far from regarding him with any distant awe, it was never thought that any sport or diversion could go on in the right way, unless *papa* were of the party, or that the rainiest day could be dull so he were at home.

He never did show much concern about regulating systematically what is usually called *education* in the case of his own children. It seemed, on the contrary, as if he attached little importance to anything else, so he could perceive that the young curiosity was excited — the intellect, by whatever springs of interest, set in motion. . . .

By many external accomplishments, either in girl or boy, he set little store. He delighted to hear his daughters to sing an old ditty, or one of his own framing; but, so the singer appeared to feel the spirit of her ballad, he was not at all critical of the technical execution. There was one thing, however, on which he fixed his heart hardly less than the ancient Persians of the Cyropaedia; like them, next to love of truth, he held love of horsemanship for the prime point of education. ... He taught them to think nothing of tumbles, and habituated them to his own reckless delight in perilous fords and flooded streams.

JOHN G. LOCKHART

What a father says to his children is not heard by the world, but it will be heard by posterity.

JEAN PAUL RICHTER

Questions

"What are atoms?" a young boy asked his father.

"I really don't know, son. All I can tell you about them is that they can't be seen."

A little later the son asked his father: "Dad, can you tell me what gravity is?"

"Well, my boy, all I can tell you is that it is some kind of force that pulls away from the earth."

After the son had futilely asked a number of other questions, he finally said, "Gee, Dad, I hope you don't mind me asking you so many questions."

"Why of course not!" exclaimed the father. "You go right ahead and ask me any questions you want. After all, if you don't ask questions how in the world are you ever going to learn anything?"

Will Rogers as Remembered by His Son

"Live in such a way that you would not be ashamed to sell your parrot to the town gossip," my father once said.

If Will Rogers had a rule to live by, maybe that's the one. Anyway, it's the one I remember best.

Many of his words are still repeated often. However, his heritage to his children wasn't words, or possessions, but an unspoken treasure, the treasure of his example as a man and a father. More than anything I have, I'm trying to pass that on to my children.

I remember my father with reverence and laughter. To many he was an Oklahoma cowboy, with a hair lick over his forehead, an infectious grin, twirling a long lariat, and speaking a language of his own that bit big chunks into the sham of his day. He's thought of as a humorist. He was, but he was more, too. He was never an actor, though his name blazed in lights from Hollywood and Broadway to Berlin and Alaska. He was always himself. Even as a wit he was trying to express ideas and ideals, and he would have preferred approval for them rather than applause for his humor.

I do not remember receiving very much lecturing from him at any time. He gave my sister Mary, my brother Jim, and me a good moral tone with the quiet sincerity which was always evident in all he said and did.

When I was a kid I wanted a motor to attach to my bike. I wanted it badly, maybe because none of the other kids had one. But it was very expensive and Father said no.

"But Dad, we're rich," I protested.

Well, the whole roof descended on me. He said no kid of his was ever going to parade any advantage he might have, and I'd better unlearn any such notions at once. Then he muttered something about show-offs, the poor show-off who is always lonely because he's always empty.

That made a big impression on me. Not so much the event, but the meaning my father gave it. Undue emphasis on material things made possessions ends in themselves, and that was morally wrong, if not destructive.

Growing up with that idea can make Christian ethics a habit, though at the time we didn't think of it that way, and my father didn't put it to us that way. The example is always more effective than the sermon. And he often put his ideas to us with a kind of barbed laughter. When any of us felt important or inflated with our knowledge, we had only to remember his remark:

"Everybody is ignorant, only on different subjects." ...

He was always the example. In those days parents assumed an automatic leadership I don't see in parents today, including myself. My father was the head of the house. He behaved as the head of the house. He was the parent, kindly, generous, but definite. When he said it should be done, it was done. That fashioned us when we were young. ...

I went to Stanford and majored in philosophy. ... One day I told my father: "That old Greek, Socrates, put it all in two simple words: 'Know thyself.' "

"Yep, and then get to know the other fellow, too," my father said. "There's always two halves to a whole."

That was pretty good for a cowboy who never got beyond the fourth grade.

He was always suspicious of any one with a pat and absolute answer to every problem. He believed in man's failure as well as his glory, and was willing to accept both, because with his compassion he knew all of us take two steps backwards before we move one step forward.

WILL ROGERS, JR.

From the Mountaintop

One of the prime factors in heading me for wherever I've gone was the fact that during my boyhood years we lived on a mountaintop in the Rockies, at ten thousand feet, where we could see in three directions for about a hundred and fifty miles. ...

Living on that mountaintop during the formative years of my life played a part in charting the course of all the years that have followed. From our mountain the world seemed to stretch out before me. ...

But my father gave me other and still greater vistas. My father had been a student of almost every subject under the sun. In some respects I think he is the most highly educated man I have ever known. Religion, philosophy, geology, zoology, botany, literature, astronomy — he studied them all. And his curiosity and enthusiasm for all things he passed on to me. He would get me up at all hours of the night, even when it was below zero, to show me things that could not be seen earlier in the night; astronomical phenomena of startling beauty in the rarefied night sky of our ten-thousand-foot eyrie.

He would point out some celestial marvel against the backdrop of the mighty mountains and, being a deeply spiritual man, he tied it all up with God. (At two or three A.M. my own boyhood reaction was not quite so spiritual!) Nevertheless, he gave me a conception of the spiritual quality of the universe that has gone with me as I have roamed the earth.

The wide range of my father's reading couldn't help but affect me. He was always a liberal in his thoughts, and was constantly seeking for new light and deeper truth. From him I acquired a tremendous concept of a tremendous God. He gave me both patience and impatience with pettiness in religion.

My friends have often remarked that I seem too interested and enthusiastic about everything. If so, then my father is to blame. He used to take me on trips, jaunts on which we talked about the origin of the earth. He had a scientific point of view, and never entertained mechanical notions about the beginning of the universe. To him it was entirely spiritual. He saw the Hand of God in everything.

LOWELL THOMAS

A Halo for Parents

If I look at a father, seeing only that he has a nose, that he is flesh and blood, with bones, limbs, skin and hair, or likewise a mother, if I do not look upon her otherwise than that, I am not seeing her at all, but trampling her under foot. But when the fourth commandment is added, then I see them adorned with a glorious crown and golden chain, which is the Word of God. And that shows you why you should honor this flesh and blood of your parents for the sake of God's Word. ... The round halo which is painted around the heads of saints is around the heads of parents too. ... This Word of power is painted around the heads of parents as a diadem, just as if the majesty and the Word of God were painted about their heads.

MARTIN LUTHER

One night a Father overheard his son pray: "Dear God, make me the kind of man my Daddy is."

Later that evening the Father prayed: "Dear God, help me to be the kind of man my son wants me to be."

Matthew Arnold, English Poet, to His Father, Famous Headmaster of Rugby School

But thou wouldst not alone
Be saved, my father! alone
Conquer and come to thy goal,
Leaving the rest in the wild.
We were weary, and we were
Fearful, and we in our march
Fain to drop down and to die.
Still thou turnest, and still
Gavest the weary thy hand.
If, in the paths of the world,
Stones might have wounded thy feet,
Toil or dejection have tried
Thy spirit, of that we saw
Nothing: to us thou wast still
Cheerful, and helpful, and firm!
Therefore to thee it was given
Many to save with thyself,
And, at the end of the day,
O faithful shepherd to come
Bringing thy sheep in thy hand. . . .
Yes! I believe that there lived
Others like thee in the past,
Not like the men of the crowd
Who all round me today
Bluster or cringe, and make life
Hideous, and arid, and vile;
But souls tempered with fire,
Fervent, heroic, and good,
Helpers and friends of mankind.

Like My Dad

Lord, make me something like my dad;
Give me a little of his will,
That good old stubborness he had
That helped him up the hardest hill,
Content to wait and work and fight,
Believing always he was right.

DOUGLAS MALLOCH

God did not make us to be eaten up by anxiety,
but to walk erect, free, unafraid in a world
where there is work to do, truth to seek,
love to give and win.

Joseph Fort Newton

IV

A Father's Fidelity

The Richness of Simplicity

My father gave me my first and best knowledge of books by his own delight and dependence upon them, and ruled my early attempts at writing by the severity and simplicity of his own good taste.

"Don't try to write *about* people and things, tell them just as they are!" ...

The old house [at North Berwick, Maine] was well provided with leather-bound books of a deeply serious nature, but in my youthful appetite for knowledge, I could even in the driest find something vital, and in the more entertaining I was completely lost.

My father has inherited from his father an amazing knowledge of human nature, and from his mother's French ancestry, that peculiarly French trait, called *gaieté de coeur*. Through all the heavy responsibilities and anxieties of his busy professional life, this kept him young at heart and cheerful. His visits to his patients were often made perfectly delightful and refreshing to them by his kind heart, and the charm of his personality.

I knew many of the patients whom he used to visit in lonely inland farms, or on the seacoast in York and Wells. I used to follow him about silently, like an understanding little dog, content to follow at his heels. ...

I cannot help believing that he recognized long before I did myself, in what direction the current of purpose in my life was setting. Now, as I write my sketches of country life, I remember again and again the wise things he said, and the sights he made me see. He was only impatient with affectation and insincerity.

The quiet village life, the dull routine of farming or mill life, early became interesting to me. I was taught to find everything that an imaginative child could ask, in the simple scene close at hand.

SARAH ORNE JEWETT

Joseph P. Kennedy and His Son, John F. Kennedy

"Little things are important," Kennedy told a reporter some years ago. "While Jack and Joe were just kids, when they were in baseball or football games, or when the girls were in a school play, no matter where I was, Washington or the West Coast or wherever, and no matter how busy I was, I'd somehow get back to see them perform. That way they know you are interested, really interested, and when you tell them something it means something." . . .

When John was a senior at the Choate School he wrote his father that he had "definitely decided to stop fooling around. . . . I really feel now that I think it over, that I have been bluffing myself about how much real work I have been doing."

In reply, Kennedy expressed "great satisfaction" over this "forthrightness and directness that you are usually lacking." . . . "Now, Jack," he wrote, "I don't want to give the impression that I am a nagger, for goodness knows I think that is the worst thing a parent can be. After long experience in sizing up people I definitely know you have the goods and you can go a long way. Now aren't you foolish not to get all there is out of what God has given you. . . . After all I would be lacking even as a friend if I did not urge you to take advantage of the qualities you have. It is very difficult to make up fundamentals that you have neglected when you were very young and that is why I am always urging you to do the best you can. I am not expecting too much and I will not be disappointed if you do not turn out to be a genius, but I think you can be a really worthwhile citizen with good judgment and good understanding." . . .

"Jack doesn't belong any more to just a family," Joseph P. Kennedy told a journalist close to his son shortly after the election. "He belongs to the country. That's probably the saddest thing about all this. The family can be there, but there is not much they can do for the President of the United States."

In the weeks before the inauguration, it almost seemed as though Joseph Kennedy were anticipating this separation and inadequacy, for he drew his family around him at every opportunity. Triumphantly he presided at the traditional Thanksgiving feast in Hyannis Port. A few days later, he visited Jack and Jackie in Georgetown following the birth of their son, John Jr. Before Christmas, when the family gathered again in Palm Beach, the new President and his father were seen together attending Mass, on the golf course, and at parties. . . .

After their long separation [during the political campaign], the press noted that father and son suddenly seemed to be together almost constantly. When a reporter asked whether this was just coincidental, Joe Kennedy's terse reply was epigrammatic. "There are no accidents in politics," he said. "I can appear with him anytime I want now." . . .

The Inauguration. Joe Kennedy, ruddy-cheeked and beaming, wore a cutaway coat, put aside twenty-one years earlier when his ambassadorship ended; it had been a source of satisfaction to him that the coat needed no alteration. . . . "This is what I've been looking forward to for a long time," Kennedy said exultantly. "It's a great day." . . . The next morning's newspapers would report that throughout the ceremony tears had glistened in Joe Kennedy's eyes. . . . As the new President's open car approached the reviewing stand outside the White House, he rose for the first and only time. Proudly his parents rose and returned his salute.

RICHARD J. WHELAN

"No Man was His Master"

The telephone would ring, sometimes quite late — "Lester, want to make a call?" Sometimes it was the first he heard the woman was going to have a baby — we took the big bag, the "obstetrical case."

"Wait downstairs," he would say when first we went on these calls. But once he called to me. The people were very poor, the woman about to give birth, no hot water in the place, no sheets.

"Here," he said, stuffing some bills in my hand, "get some coal, get some sheets."

A hundred times through the years I was sent for food or coal.

"Nothing wrong with these people," he sometimes said, "except that they're hungry."

He would stop at a grocery and send over an order.

I would not say my father gave away as much as he took in, but there is some chance of it. My father died broke; and I am proud of it.

It was in medicine that his heart went out to humanity, and that he could do something in a practical way. Here there was no waiting for the "cooperative commonwealth"; this was a case of, "Boy, run down to the drugstore and call an ambulance." (The people had no phone.) Or, "Boy, out for more bandages —" he was staunching the flow, the bandages in his bag were being exhausted.

At these moments he felt the close and living connection with the best in him. . . .

Hyman had that quality that he walked alone, that no man was his master, that as he scanned the passing throng on Michigan Boulevard, his eyes tilted to the sky, he was figuring out the relationship between "man and God." (He saw God in a dream, now and again, and they would talk.)

He felt himself of the Hebrew prophets, and some part of his spirit dwelled among them. . . .

He was so much fun. I loved my father. I miss him more than anyone I ever knew.

I loved his blunt upturning nose, with the sharpest scent there ever was. His musing, bemused full mouth. Those particularly "human" eyes. The most beautiful hands you ever saw, and boy, could they percuss a chest!

LESTER COHEN

Charles Sedgwick to His Son, Charles, Jr.

Lenox, Mass. September 19, 1837

I should have answered your letter before, but I have not before today been in possession of ten dollars, which I enclose to you with pleasure. You do not say what you want it for, but I send it to you that you may have the option of declining to use it. I consider it one of the greatest uses for money for a young person to have it, and yet from sense, judgment and principle, to resist those temptations to which the young generally yield. Perhaps you will think the sum rather too small to give dignity to this moral, but to tell you the truth it is half I have, and the residue I want today. I think I can safely promise to procure and forward for your use all that you express a deliberate wish to have. I do not mean to go halfway with you in my confidence. My *reliance* is on your character, your generous and disinterested disposition, your confidence in my affection, your determination to do the right thing, knowing my circumstances and that there is nothing that I wish to conceal from you. It is, if not my greatest, certainly one of my greatest pleasures to believe your virtue is strong, that it is not dependent so much on the guardianship and vigilance of your friends, as on your own clear apprehension of right and your fixed principles.

My Father Was a King

My father was a benevolent king in our home. His royal robe was a sheepskin coat in winter, blue denim in summer, collar and tie and neat suit on Sunday. He sat at the head of the table at mealtime; his handsome head bent at night over his book or paper. His presence gave us a feeling of security, warmth and dignity. . . .

Our farm was a rolling expanse of fields, trees, and little streams of water. . . . Father gave us a sense of excitement. The early sun would come mistily over the fields and woods and little streams of water, and without benefit of alarm clock my father would be outside taking care of things. . . .

Father gave us reverence. He reverenced the new days, disliking to see lamps lit when the sun was already doing duty. "You'll burn a hole in the new day," he'd say. He reverenced thunderstorms, rains, harvests.

Father gave us peace. The peace of our kingdom's regime included a sense of wealth. There was a beautiful table with fresh butter, milk, bread, vegetables, fruit. A strange combination of frugality and largesse mixed without quarreling. . . . Perhaps the wealth was most of all in our freedom and dignity. . . .

In my father's little kingdom everyone was important, with work to do. We were praised and helped. My father would listen to my mother as she read the papers which had rated good grades at school. He submitted happily to the musical concerts which we gave freely in the days when we were learning to play the clarinet and trombone. He cared about everything we did.

It never really occurred to me that we were poor. In all the books we read, being poor meant being without things to make us happy. . . .

I always knew it was good to grow up in my father's little kingdom where violets along fence rows were not plowed up; where everything had preciousness; where Jesus was a vital personality, the center of us all. ... I always knew it was good to grow up where so much faith and love prevailed. I always knew it was a proud thing. Often, seeing us walking home from our little town with sugar or thread, people would give us rides. And when they asked our names, we loved to say whose daughters we were.

But upon reflection now, the greatest compliment to my father's castle is, I think, that it was such a great joy to grow up there.

SISTER MARY FAITH, O.S.B.

A Man's Responsibility

What it takes to be a real "he-man" in modern society is no longer the physical intrepidity of the soldier or frontiersman in the past.

What modern man is called upon to be and do requires moral courage of a high order, tenacity, patience, a deep sense of responsibility, and the willingness to endure boredom, fatigue and tensions that can be only occasionally relieved.

The real he-man, it seems to me, is not the one who takes to the woods (except, perhaps, as a relaxing week-end off once in a while), but the one who feels a quiet and deep pride in taking care of his family as a man ought to.

Sitting home at night, reading a book, while the children are tucked in their beds, it can be immensely gratifying to reflect that the whole structure of their safety and welfare depends upon one man, his work, his reliability, his responsibility, his refusal to funk his obligations.

SYDNEY J. HARRIS

Efficiency Expert

Dad was a tall man, with a large head, jowls, and a Herbert Hoover collar. He was no longer slim; he had passed the two-hundred-pound mark during his early thirties, and left it so far behind that there were times when he had to resort to railway baggage scales to ascertain his displacement. But he carried himself with the self-assurance of a successful gentleman who was proud of his wife, proud of his family, and proud of his business accomplishments.

Dad had enough gall to be divided into three parts, and the ability and poise to backstop the front he placed before the world. He'd walk into a factory like the Zeiss works in Germany or the Pierce Arrow plant in this country and announce that he could speed up production by one fourth. He'd do it, too.

One reason he had so many children — there were twelve of us — was that he was convinced anything he and Mother teamed up on was sure to be a success.

Dad always practiced what he preached, and it was just about impossible to tell where his scientific management company ended and his family life began. His office was always full of children, and he often took two or three of us, and sometimes all twelve, on business trips. Frequently, we'd tag along at his side, pencils and notebooks in our hands, when Dad toured a factory which had hired him as an efficiency expert.

On the other hand, our house at Montclair, New Jersey, was a sort of school for scientific management and the elimination of wasted motions — or "motion study" as Dad and Mother named it.

Dad took loving pictures of us children washing dishes, so that he could figure out how we could reduce our motions and thus hurry through the task. Irregular jobs, such as painting the back porch or removing a stump from the front lawn, were awarded on a low-bid basis. Each child who wanted extra pocket money submitted a sealed bid saying what he would do the job for. The lowest bidder got the contract. ...

Yes, at home or on the job, Dad was always the efficiency expert. He buttoned his vest from the bottom up, instead of from the top down, because the bottom-to-top took him only three seconds, while the top-to-bottom took seven. He even used two shaving brushes to lather his face, because he found that by so doing he could cut seventeen seconds off the shaving time. ...

Dad was happiest in a crowd, especially a crowd of kids. Wherever he was, you'd see a string of them trailing him — and the ones with plenty of freckles were pretty sure to be Gilbreths.

He had a way with children and knew how to keep them on their toes. He had a respect for them, too, and didn't mind showing it. ...

Really, it was love of children more than anything else that made him want a pack of his own. Even with a dozen, he wasn't fully satisfied. Sometimes he'd look us over and say to Mother: "Never you mind, Lillie. You did the best you could." ...

Whenever Dad returned from a trip — even if he had been gone only a day — he whistled the family "assembly call" as he turned in at the sidewalk of our large brown home in Montclair. ...

So when we heard him whistle, we never knew whether to expect good news or bad, rags or riches. But we did know for sure we'd better get there in a hurry.

Sometimes, as we all came running to the front door, he'd start by being stern.

"Let me see your nails, all of you," he'd grunt, with his face screwed up in a terrible frown. "Are they clean? Have you been biting them? Do they need trimming?"

Then out would come leather manicure sets for the girls and pocket knives for the boys. How we loved him then, when his frown wrinkles reversed their field and became a wide grin.

Or he'd shake hands solemnly all around, and when you took your hand away there'd be a nut chocolate bar in it. Or he'd ask who had a pencil, and then hand out a dozen automatic ones.

FRANK GILBRETH, JR. AND ERNESTINE GILBRETH CARY

And he shall turn the heart of the fathers to the children, and the heart of the children to their fathers.

MALACHI 4, 6

The Village Blacksmith

Under a spreading chestnut tree
The village smithy stands;
The smith, a mighty man is he,
With large and sinewy hands;
And the muscles of his brawny arms
Are strong as iron bands.

His hair is crisp, and black, and long,
His face is like the tan;
His brow is wet with honest sweat,
He earns whate'er he can,
And looks the whole world in the face,
For he owes not any man. . . .

He goes on Sunday to the church,
And sits among his boys;
He hears the parson pray and preach,
He hears his daughter's voice,
Singing in the village choir,
And it makes his heart rejoice.

It sounds to him like her mother's voice,
Singing in Paradise!
He needs must think of her once more,
How in the grave she lies;
And with his hard, rough hand he wipes
A tear out of his eyes.

Toiling, — rejoicing, — sorrowing,
Onward through life he goes;
Each morning sees some task begin,
Each evening sees it close;
Something attempted, something done,
Has earned a night's repose.

Thanks, thanks to thee, my worthy friend,
For the lesson thou hast taught!
Thus at the flaming forge of life
Our fortunes must be wrought;
Thus on its sounding anvil shaped,
Each burning deed and thought!

HENRY WADSWORTH LONGFELLOW

"Holy Father"

No one has bothered to list male saints under the category of "holy father". . . . But throughout my life I have been lucky enough to know many a holy father of a family whose life was in the pattern of those who think first of the importance of their homes and the value of strong, well-trained children.

DANIEL A. LORD

Fatherhood Is Worth the Agony

I spanked my small son this morning. He looked outraged as the blows fell, and halfway through he ordered, "Stop hitting me." Then he stalked into his room, slammed the door, and climbed into his crib. A second later, I could hear him sobbing.

The offense was heinous; he had again hit his younger sister. But she did not thank me for my intervention; when I left the house, she withheld her customary hug and kiss, and even my wife withdrew a psychological step or two.

It was not the first time fatherhood had plunged me into isolation. By the nature of his duties, by the attitude of strength that he is forced to assume, the father is forever a little bit alone, even when his children are jumping on his stomach.

When he retreats to wrestle with the checkbook, he stands alone in the face of financial disaster. He must find the money for the bills, and he must make it look easy. His children and his wife must believe that their home is safe and secure as Mt. Ararat. Never by so much as a complaint or a furrowed brow, may they be permitted to glimpse the frailties of the bumbling male who is their sole defense against the world. . . .

The father must be a giant. He must be the tallest (he changes the bulbs in the ceiling fixtures), the strongest (he hauls the furniture from one floor to another), and the fastest (he pursues the errant child across busy intersections). . . .

The father must run a taut ship and stand as final authority in home discipline. After eight hours of subservience at the office, bullied by colleagues and browbeaten by his boss, he must enter his home with the commanding, judicial mien of Gen. Robert E. Lee. . . .

The father, when you come right down to it, is a fake. In the face of all the wisdom, bravery, strength, endurance, and calmness demanded, how could it be otherwise? Yet he pursues his dogged way, living up to the impossible demands of fatherhood as well as he is able and, to his astonishment, making it stick more often than not. If he is a fraud, he is at least a well-intentioned fraud, and providence helps protect those with a kindly heart.

In one respect, moreover, the father does not have to pretend at all. A father is affectionate, and this part cómes easily. At times his heart turns over and his throat contracts with a surge of love. His little girl, encased in woolly pajamas, may sing quaveringly, "Sing-a-song-a sis pence, a-pock-a-full-a rye." His son, 10 cent store helmet pulled low over his eyes, will march up, salute, and crawl onto his lap. Or both may clamber up him as if he were a ladder, their muddy shoes scrabbling against his trousers and their chocolate-covered fingers clamping tight on his white collar. At moments like this, fatherhood is worth the agony.

RIDGELY HUNT

Epitaph on My Father

O ye, whose cheek the tear of pity stains,
  Draw near with pious rev'rence, and attend!
Here lie the loving husband's dear remains,
  The tender father, and the gen'rous friend.
The pitying heart that felt for human woe,
  The dauntless heart that fear'd no human pride,
The friend of man — to vice alone a foe;
  For ev'n his failings lean'd to virtue's side.

ROBERT BURNS

Happy in the Happiness of Others

How delightful it is to recall the innocent feelings of
unbounded love, confidence, and respect, associated with
my earliest visions of my parents. ... Always visibly
happy in the happiness of others, especially of children,
our father entered into all our pleasures, and soothed and
cheered us in all our little griefs with such overflowing
tenderness, that it was no wonder we almost worshipped
him. My first recollection of him is of his carrying me
up to his private room to prayers, in the summer evenings,
about sunset, and rewarding my silence and attention
afterwards with a view of the flower-garden through his
prism. Then I recall the delight it was to me to be permitted to sleep with him during a confinement of my
mother's — how I longed for the morning, because then
he would be sure to tell me some fairy tale, of his own
invention, all sparkling with gold and diamonds, magic
fountains and enchanted princesses. In the eyes of memory
I can still see him as he was at that period of his life, —
his fatherly countenance, unmixed with any of the less
lovable expressions that, in too many faces, obscure the
character — but preeminently *fatherly;* conveying the
idea of kindness, intellect and purity; his manner grave,
manly and cheerful, in unison with his high and open
forehead; his very attitudes, whether as he sat absorbed
in the arrangement of his minerals, shells and insects —
or as he labored in his garden until his naturally pale
complexion acquired a tinge of fresh healthy red; or as,
coming lightly towards us with some unexpected present,
his smile of indescribable benevolence spoke exultation
in the foretaste of our rapture.

GEORGE CRABBE

So It's a Girl

Many of my non-Jewish friends want to know all about the business of the Jews' always praying, "May it be a boy." The religious Jew wanted his first born to be a boy, of course. A boy says Kaddish, the prayer of mourning for the parents after they are dead. It was merely a question of substituting terms. What they really meant and often said was, "Thank God for one-who'll-say-Kaddish."

. . .

I remember when my younger brother's wife, Annie, was in the hospital for her first baby. It was a girl. My brother Max immediately put through a call to my father and it was a delightful conversation:

Max: Hello, Pop, well, Annie had the baby and Annie is in fine shape.

Pop: All right, let's thank God everything is all right.

Max: Oh yes, everything is fine, Annie is fine.

Pop: This is very good news, my son.

Max: Oh yes, Annie is fine.

Finally my father busted loose: What's the matter with you? It's not so bad! Suppose *it is* a little girl, so what? It's not so terrible. . . .

Max: Annie is fine. . . .

HARRY GOLDEN

Fathers who share their children's growing time cannot grow old. . . . Who would not hold fast to the hand placed so confidingly within his own, leading and being led towards great visions and rich venturing? All the old failures must be made good for the child's sake. All weakness is to be strengthened that he may be strong.

ANGELO PATRI

From St. Thomas More's Last Letter to His Daughter, before His Execution

Our Lord bless you, good daughter, and your good husband, and your little boy, and all my children, and all my Godchildren and all our friends. . . . Tomorrow long I go to God; it were a day very meet and convenient for me. I never liked your manner toward me better than when you kissed me last: for I love when daughterly love and dear charity hath no leisure to look on worldly courtesy. Fare well my dear child, and pray for me, and I shall for you and all your friends, that we may merrily meet in heaven.

The Man's Prayer

When all is still within these walls,
And Thy sweet sleep through darkness falls
On little hearts that trust in me,
However bitter toil may be,
For length of days, O Lord! on Thee,
*   My spirit calls.*

Their daily need by day enthralls
My hand and brain, but when night falls
And leaves the questioning spirit free
To brood upon the days to be,
For time and strength, O Lord! on Thee
*   My spirit calls.*

T. A. DALY

The Christian renewal will take place only if the father, the head of the Christian home, regains effective spiritual leadership.

WILLIAM S. MORRIS

I have no doubt that my father's vivid reading of Biblical stories planted in my impressionable mind a reverence and respect for the Bible, perhaps even a sense of its dramatic values, which in subsequent years was to turn me to the Great Book for themes to thrill motion picture audiences.

CECIL B. DEMILLE

The Bridge Builder

An old man, going a lone highway,
Came at the evening, cold and gray,
To a chasm, vast and deep and wide,
Through which was flowing a sullen tide.
The old man crossed in the twilight dim;
The sullen stream had no fears for him;
But he turned when safe on the other side
And built a bridge to span the tide.

"Old man," said a fellow pilgrim near,
"You are wasting strength with building here;
Your journey will end with the ending day;
You never again must pass this way;
You have crossed the chasm, deep and wide —
Why build you at the eventide?"

The builder lifted his old gray head:
"Good friend, in the path I have come," he said,
"There followeth after me today
A youth whose feet must pass this way.
This chasm that has been naught to me
To that fair-haired youth may a pitfall be.
He, too, must cross in the twilight dim;
Good friend, I am building the bridge for him."

WILL ALLEN DRUMGOOLE

Acknowledgments

The compiler and the publisher gratefully acknowledge the permission of the following publishers and copyright owners for the use of the protected material indicated:

AMERICAN LEGION MAGAZINE, from Daniel A. Poling's article, issue of November, 1948.

BETTER HOMES AND GARDENS, for quotation by Burton Hillis.

JOSEPH H. BREIG, from his *A Halo for Father*, copyright, 1954, by The Bruce Publishing Co.

CHILTON BOOKS, from Lester Cohen's *Mom and Pop — A Portrait*, copyright, 1963, by Lester Cohen.

COLUMBIA UNIVERSITY PRESS, from *Letters of Emerson*, edited by Robert L. Rusk.

CONCEPTION ABBEY PRESS, Conception, Mo., from Sister Mary Faith, O.S.B., in *Altar and Home*, December, 1956.

MRS. KENNETH C. CRAIN, for Mrs. Burton Rascoe, from Burton Rascoe's *Before I Forget*, copyright, 1937, by Burton Rascoe.

THOMAS Y. CROWELL CO., from *Cheaper by the Dozen*, by Frank Gilbreth, Jr. and Ernestine Gilbreth Cary, copyright, 1948, by Frank Gilbreth, Jr. and Ernestine Gilbreth Cary.

RICHARD CARDINAL CUSHING, for his "My Father's Three Words" in *Parade Magazine*, January 8, 1956.

DOUBLEDAY AND CO., INC., from *Family Gathering* by Kathleen Norris, copyright, © 1959, by Kathleen Norris, reprinted by permission of Doubleday and Co., Inc.

DR. WILL DURANT, from his article in *Ladies Home Journal*, 1946.

E. P. DUTTON AND CO., INC., for "My Father" from *Homer's Golden Chain* by Virginia Moore, copyright, 1936, by E. P. Dutton and Co., Inc., renewal © 1964 by Virginia Moore.

FORTRESS PRESS, from Martin Luther's *Sermons on the Catechism*, in *Luther's Works*, translated by J. W. Doberstein, copyright, 1959, by Fortress Press.

GUIDEPOSTS MAGAZINE, from Will Rogers, Jr.'s tribute to his father in *Guideposts to a Stronger Faith*, ed. by Norman Vincent Peale, reprinted from *Guideposts Magazine*, copyright, 1959, Guideposts Associates, Carmel, N. Y.